Dave Lambert

The Creature in the Night

Ernst Klett Verlag
Stuttgart Düsseldorf Leipzig

Zu dieser Lektüre gibt es eine Kassette
(Klettnummer 570961)

9 783125 709607

1. Auflage A 1 10 9 | 2007

Alle Drucke dieser Auflage können im Unterricht nebeneinander benutzt werden. Die letzte Zahl bezeichnet das Jahr dieses Druckes.

Internetadresse: http://www.klett-verlag.de

Zeichnungen: Peter Gray, London.
Druck: Druckhaus Vogel, Echterdingen.
Printed in Germany.
ISBN 3-12-570960-1

Contents

Chapter 1: Noises in the night

It was *my* idea to go camping that summer. Now I sometimes think it was a bad idea because many strange things happened on that camping holiday …

My sister Kelly and I met our cousins Lucy and Toby at the train station and took the train to Eastbourne and then a bus. When we arrived at Home Farm, the farmer showed us a big field and told us we could put up our two tents there. It was a really beautiful place! The road on one side was very quiet because there was no traffic. There were woods on two sides of the field and a lake at one end. Behind the lake there were some hills. There were no other campers, just a French family in a caravan under a big tree in the middle of the field. On the other side of the lake, we could see a small tent, all alone. There was a small boat next to it.

"There's no problem with cows or sheep," the farmer told us, "I don't put my animals in this field. You can come up to the house if you need something: showers, water, fresh milk and eggs for breakfast. It's only about half a mile away, behind that hill. Well, happy camping! Come on, Sheppy!" And his little dog followed him.

2	**strange** [streɪndʒ]	seltsam, komisch
4	**cousin** ['kʌzn]	Vetter; Kusine
12	**caravan** ['kærəvæn]	Wohnwagen
13	**other** ['ʌðə]	andere, -r, -s
20	**come on**!	komm' (mit)!

We started to put up our two small tents next to the lake where we could get water and swim. That first night we had a fantastic barbecue: chicken-burgers, crisps, chocolate bars and lemonade. After our meal, we sat around the campfire. My sister Kelly had her guitar and so we sang some songs. I didn't know it could be so dark in the country! The French family's caravan was in total darkness. On the other side of the lake it was foggy. We couldn't see a thing!

"It's spooky here!" said Toby. "Who knows a good ghost story? This is a great place for it."

"Who is in that little tent on the other side of the lake?" asked my sister, Kelly. "I haven't seen anybody there all evening. And there is no light ..."

"That's because a ghost lives there," said Toby. "He stays in all day and only comes out at night when it's dark and foggy."

"Oh, Toby!" said Lucy. "I'm really scared now!" And she started to make ghost noises. "Ooooo! Ooooooooo!" – she just wanted to show she wasn't afraid.

Suddenly, there was a terrible noise. It seemed to be right next to us in the trees. "Ooooo! Ooooooooo!" We all jumped!

"Oh! What was that?" said Lucy.

4	**we sat** [sæt]	wir saßen
5	**campfire** ['kæmpfaɪə]	Lagerfeuer
5	**so**	*hier:* also, deshalb
5	**we sang**	wir sangen
8	**darkness** ['dɑ:knɪs]	Dunkelheit, Finsternis
13	**I haven't seen anybody**	ich habe niemanden gesehen
22	**right next to us**	direkt neben uns

"Just an owl … I think," I said. "In that tree."

And we all laughed because we felt so silly. It was late and we were tired, so we lit the camping gas lamp between our tents and got into our sleeping bags. I was in a tent with Toby, and Lucy was with my sister.

In the night, Toby had a great idea.

"Hey, James! Let's scare the girls!" he said. We left our tent quietly and went to the girls' tent. We listened: they were still talking.

"It's so dark here!"

"Are you scared, Lucy?"

"Well … yes. I didn't know this was just a farm. I thought it was a normal camping site. You know, with shops and a lot of people."

"Yes, me too. But now we've got a dark field, one French family and one empty tent on the other side of the lake."

"Mmmm … spooky!"

Toby and I thought this was a good time to make some noises. "Oo-oo-oo-ooo!"

"D-did you hear that?" whispered Lucy.

"It must be that owl again," said Kelly.

"But this time it's different … and it's right next to our tent! W-who's there?"

1 **owl** [aʊl]	Eule
2 **we felt**	wir fühlten (uns) …
3 **we lit**	wir zündeten ... an
3 **lamp**	Lampe
4 **we got into …**	*hier:* wir schlüpften … hinein
7 **scare**	erschrecken
8 **quietly**	leise

"Oo-oo-oo-ooo!" We made the noise again.

"Do you think it's a farm animal?" whispered Lucy. "This *is* a farm ..."

"Perhaps," said Kelly. "But the farmer said he doesn't put animals in this field, remember?"

"That's true. Perhaps it's a wild animal from the woods!"

Toby and I wanted to laugh. Perhaps the girls heard us.

"James? Toby? Is that you out there?"

"Ha! We scared you! We scared you!" we shouted.

The girls were angry. "We knew it was you all the time, silly boys! We weren't afraid!"

"You were! We heard you! You thought it was a wild animal! Or perhaps you thought it was the ghost from that tent over there! Ha, ha!"

"Go to bed, you two!" Kelly said. "We're tired."

Toby and I got into our sleeping bags. We were still laughing about the girls. Suddenly, there was a sound outside our tent. It was right next to our heads. It was a strange sound. "Ruhhhhh ... Ruhhhhh ... Shhhhh."

"What did you say?" I asked Toby.

"I didn't say anything," he answered.

Everything was quiet for a long time. Then we heard the strange sound again. "Ruhhhhh ... Ruhhhhh ... Shhhhh."

"Don't snore!" said Toby.

"I'm not snoring!" I whispered. "How can I be snoring? I'm not sleeping!"

7	**they heard** [hɜ:d]	sie hörten
10	**we knew** [nju:]	wir wussten
21	**I didn't say anything**	ich sagte nichts, ich habe nichts gesagt
24	**snore** [snɔ:]	schnarchen

"Well … what's that strange sound?" whispered Toby.

"It's just the girls. They think they can scare *us*, now. Okay, girls!" I shouted. "We know you're out there!"

"Ruhhhh … Ruhhhhhh! Shhhhh!"

The terrible sound came again. It was very loud this time, as if something very big was breathing outside the tent.

"Hey, I know! Perhaps it's the farmer's dog," said Toby.

But I knew Sheppy could not make that noise, and I knew she was up at Home Farm. She was barking and I could hear her. A big shadow from the lamp moved across the tent. A very big shadow. It was like the shadow of a big wild animal. Toby and I were very scared. One thing we knew: that was *not* Sheppy.

5	**loud** [laʊd]	laut
6	**as if something was breathing**	als ob etwas gerade atmete
10	**(Sheppy) was barking**	(Sheppy) bellte gerade

Chapter 2: At Home Farm

Well, of course, we didn't sleep very well after that. In the morning, Toby and I asked the girls about the strange sound in the night.

"The owl?" they asked.

"No, after that, there was another noise ..." we said. "Like this: Ruhhhh ... Ruhhhhh ... Shhhhhhh!"

"More strange noises?" they laughed. "Oh, stop it, you two!"

"Well, what about the big shadow from the gas lamp?"

"What shadow? You've played enough tricks, boys!" said Kelly. "Let's go up to Home Farm and buy some eggs and milk for breakfast. I'm hungry!"

So it wasn't the girls. Or perhaps they were acting very well. The French family were having breakfast outside their caravan. With the binoculars, we looked at the other side of the lake. Outside the little tent, an old man was sitting next to the lake. He was fishing.

"There's your ghost, Toby," said Lucy and laughed. "Only an old fisherman! Come on, let's go up to Home Farm!"

I went behind our tent to get my trainers. But they weren't there!

"Hey! Who's got my trainers?" I asked. "I put them here behind our tent last night."

1 **very well** *hier:* sehr gut
7 **more** (noch) mehr
10 **enough** [ɪ'nʌf] genug
19 **fisherman** Fischer
21 **to get** *hier:* um zu holen

“Why do you leave them outside all night, James?” asked Lucy.

“Have you slept in a small tent with James’s trainers?” Toby asked Lucy.

“Oh, I see,” said Lucy with her hand to her nose.

“Where are they?” I shouted. “I left them there last night and now they’re gone!”

We looked everywhere, inside the tents, in the field and under the trees in the woods. “Someone has stolen them!” I said.

“Or some*thing* has stolen them …” said Toby. We were thinking of the big shadow in the night.

“What’s this?” said Lucy. She was looking at something white in the grass between the tents. “Look! There’s a lot of it!”

“Sheep’s wool?,” said Toby.

“That’s not sheep’s wool,” we all said. “It’s hair! Animal hair!” But we didn’t know which animal. And we didn’t know why it was there.

“Do you think … perhaps this furry white animal … stole my trainers?” I asked my friends.

“Well, this furry animal could climb,” said Lucy. “Look, there’s a fence around this field!”

“Perhaps it flew in …”

3 **have you slept?**	hast du geschlafen?
8 **inside**	innerhalb, in
9 **someone has stolen** ['stəʊlən] **them**	jemand hat sie gestohlen
16 **wool** [wʊl]	Wolle
20 **furry** ['fɜːrɪ] **animal**	Pelztier; struppiges/haariges Tier
23 **fence** [fens]	Zaun

"What? So you think a furry white creature climbed or flew into this field last night and stole James's smelly old pair of trainers!" laughed Kelly. "You're all crazy!"

"Those trainers were new," I said.

When we arrived at Home Farm my feet were hurting. It was only half a mile, but without shoes, it was more like ten miles. The farmer was there. He was wearing a flat cap and green wellingtons. With him was a young boy of sixteen.

"This is Bart, my sister's boy. Bart's helping me on the farm for the summer."

Bart was very tall. He had black hair and he was wearing a *Chicago Bulls* baseball cap. He did not say hello.

"Did you sleep well?" the farmer asked.

"Oh, er … not bad," we said.

"It must be very dark out there in that field for you city kids," the farmer laughed.

"Yes, very dark," we said. "But we have a gas lamp, so it's okay."

The farmer went to get the eggs and the milk. Bart didn't look at us, but asked, "Did you see the old man in the tent on the other side of the lake?"

"Well, we saw him this morning," we said. "Last night when we went to bed the tent was in darkness. There was no light on."

1	**creature** ['kriːtʃə]	Wesen, Kreatur
2	**smelly**	übelriechend, stinkend
3	**crazy** ['kreɪzɪ]	verrückt
7	**flat**	flach
8	**wellingtons (wellies)**	Gummistiefel
12	**tall** [tɔːl]	groß

"That's because he's not in his tent at night," said Bart.

"Really? Well … where does he sleep?" we asked.

"He doesn't sleep. He walks around …"

"He walks around at night?" we asked. "Why?"

Bart looked around. "Because he's a weirdo …"

"A weirdo?"

"That's what people say," said Bart. "Sometimes he comes round the lake and walks around the camping site. My uncle doesn't tell people about him, of course … But you mustn't talk to him! He's dangerous! A real weirdo!"

The farmer came back with our eggs and some fresh milk.

"You can't buy food as fresh as this in town!" he laughed. "That's £2.50. Hey, where are your trainers, my boy?" He looked down at my feet.

5 **weirdo** ['wɪədəʊ] *(informal)*	verrückter Typ, komischer Kerl
9 **uncle** ['ʌŋkl]	Onkel
10 **real**	echt, wirklich

"Oh … I … er … lost them," I answered, embarrassed.

"James thinks somebody stole them from behind the tent," said Kelly.

"Well, I put them out last night and in the morning they were gone!" I said.

"Did you hear somebody when you were in your tents last night?" asked Bart.

"Well," I said. "It seems crazy now, but Toby and I heard a strange noise right next to our tent."

"And we saw a shadow," said Toby. "A big shadow!"

The farmer said, "And you say you heard a noise?"

Toby and I tried to make the noise. We were very embarrassed because now everyone was laughing at us.

"*We* didn't hear it or see it," the girls told the farmer. Thanks a lot, girls!

"You city kids are just scared of the dark," laughed the farmer. "No animals can get into that field. There's a fence around it."

"But somebody … or something stole my trainers!" I said.

"Wasn't there a story about a … a creature in this part of the country, Uncle Dick?" asked Bart.

"What creature? Oh, that was only an old story, Bart."

"Tell us about this … creature!" we asked the farmer.

But he just laughed, "Well, it's just a silly old story, but some people say there is a creature in this part of the country. They say it comes in the night and steals sheep and … small children. And then eats them! They say it's

12 **we tried** [traɪd] wir versuchten

very dangerous. It's more than seven feet tall! But I can see I'm scaring you kids! Nobody has *seen* the creature."

"What does this creature look like?" we asked the farmer.

"Well, they say it's furry," said the farmer. "It has long hair."

"What … c-colour is its hair?" we asked, really scared now.

"White," he answered. "But don't be afraid. There is no creature. It's just an old story. Now come on, Bart," he said. "It's time to kill those chickens."

On our way back to the camping site, we talked about what the farmer and Bart had told us. The creature had white hair, just like the hair Lucy found that morning! And what about the weirdo? Did he really walk around the camping site at night? Toby and Lucy wanted to go to another camping site. I just wanted another pair of trainers. Suddenly, Kelly stopped.

"Wait!" she said. "There's something the farmer said. I don't understand it. I'm going back to ask him."

We arrived back at the farm. Bart and the farmer were going into the barn. "We're going to kill some chickens," he said. "Do you want to watch?"

Kelly said she was sorry, but we forgot to buy a small bottle of camping gas.

1	**more than**	mehr als
2	**nobody** [ˈnəʊbədɪ]	niemand
11	**kill**	töten, umbringen; *hier:* schlachten
11	**chickens** [ˈtʃɪkɪnz]	Hühner
14	**just like**	genau wie
14	**she found** [faʊnd]	sie fand
22	**barn** [bɑːn]	Scheune

"Bart, wait here for me and don't open the barn door." The farmer left Bart next to the barn and went to find the camping gas.

"Thank you," said Kelly when he came back. "We need it for our lamp tonight … Oh, there's something I want to ask you, please."

"Yes … ?" said the farmer.

"You saw my brother had no shoes …"

"That's right. It's not a good idea to walk in the country without shoes! There are cows, you know!" he laughed.

Kelly did not laugh. "You said *'Where are your trainers?'* "

"That's right. And … ?"

"Well, I don't understand," said Kelly. "How did you know my brother had trainers?"

The farmer looked at Kelly with big eyes. How *did* he know I had trainers, not shoes or boots or sandals?

"Uncle Dick! Uncle Dick!" It was Bart. "Quick! The chickens are outside … I can't … !"

"Oh, that boy!" said the farmer. "He's opened the barn door! I have to go and help him! Sorry!" He ran back to the barn. All the farmer's chickens were running around outside!

22 **they were running** sie rannten gerade

Chapter 3: A bad dream?

When we arrived back at our tents, we had a wonderful breakfast. It was a beautiful day, so we planned a hike in the hills and woods. Toby had a pair of walking boots, so I had something to wear on my feet. We packed a picnic of cheese sandwiches, crisps, apples and lemonade. Then we closed our tents and started to walk. The French family were still sitting under the tree outside their caravan in the middle of the field. They waved to us and we waved back.

"Perhaps they heard or saw something strange last night. Let's ask them!" I said.

The French family did not speak a lot of English, but I think in the end they understood what we were saying.

"Hello," I started. "Nice day … Did you all sleep well?"

"Oh, yes!" said the father. "Very well!" He was small and wore a red cap.

"Good … You didn't see a big shadow? In the gas lamp?"

"Gas … lamp?" said the father, and his wife said something to him in French. "Ahhh … !" and he went into the caravan. When he came out, he was carrying a gas lamp. "For you!" he said. "No problem, we have three!"

"No, no!" said Lucy. "Thank you, but you don't understand. We don't need a gas lamp …"

"Did you hear a strange noise last night?" I asked. The father looked at me. Then he looked at the mother. Then they said something in French to the three children and then the father looked back at us again.

2 **hike** Wanderung
7 **they were still sitting** sie saßen noch
8 **to wave** [weɪv] winken

"What ...?" he said. He took off his red cap and tried to understand.

"Last night ... did you ... hear something? A strange creature, perhaps?"

"Last ... night ...?" they said. They did not understand. In the end, Toby made a noise like the creature: "Ruhhhhhh ... Shhhhhhhh!" and said, "A furry creature !"

"Furry?" said the father.

"Yes! A big furry thing!" we all said together.

"Big?" said the father.

"Yes, yes! Very big!" we said. "More than seven feet tall!"

"Ah! ... And ... and white?" he asked.

"Yes, that's right! They say it has white hair!" we shouted. So he knew! Perhaps it came to their caravan in the night too!

"Ah, oui!" said the father and the mother together. They understood! "Furry! Very big!" and they put their hands up to show us it was very big. "And white!" Then the father

16 **Ah, oui!** [ɑ: wi:] *(French)* Oh, yes!

made a noise just like the terrible animal. “Ruhhhhh! … Ruhhhhh! Shhhhh!” He was very good.

“Yes, yes!” we all shouted. We weren’t crazy! Other people heard the creature and saw it too. I tried to tell them in easy English: Toby and I saw the creature’s shadow and it stole my trainers. But the French family just looked at us. The father said again ‘furry’ and ‘very big’ and ‘white’ and showed us his watch.

“Why … why is he showing us his watch?” said Lucy.

“I don’t know, but I think he’s saying … it could come again tonight!” said Toby.

We stopped at a river for our picnic and hiked in the hills in the afternoon. But it wasn’t fun because we could only think about the creature. Perhaps the French family was right: it *could* come again in the night. Toby, Lucy and I wanted to get back to the camping site before it was dark. But my sister Kelly didn’t think there was a creature.

“What do you think it can be, then, Kelly? Do you think it’s the weirdo?” I asked.

“Perhaps,” said Kelly.

“You still think it’s the farmer,” I said.

“Well, how did he know you had trainers?” said Kelly.

We didn’t know the answer to that question.

“Hmmm … ,” said Toby. “It could be the Frenchman. He makes very good animal noises.”

When we arrived back at the camping site, it was almost dark. The French family were going to bed. Lucy took the binoculars and looked at the other side of the lake.

14–15 **the family was right** die Familie hatte Recht

“Look!” she said. “There is no light in the tent over there. And it’s all closed up.” We did not say anything. But we were all thinking the same thing.

That night we had a very quick meal. We did not sit around the campfire and we did not sing songs. We lit the gas lamp and put it between our tents. Then we got into our sleeping bags – fast.

I was having a bad dream. A monster opened the door of our tent. It had white hair, a baseball cap and green wellingtons. It said something to me in French: “Ruhhhhh … Ruhhhhh … Shhhhh!” It was terrible! So I did what I always do in bad dreams and said, “It’s only a dream, James. It’s only a dream.” But then I heard Toby. He was whispering: “It isn’t a dream, James! This is really happening!”

I opened my eyes. Toby looked very scared! His eyes were big and his mouth was open.

“It’s out there! It *has* come back!”

We listened. Something or somebody was there: it was breathing right next to our heads. Was it the weirdo from the tent on the other side of the lake? Was it the big furry white creature? Then we saw the shadow again. In the light from the gas lamp, it was very big. It was walking around between our tents and it was breathing: “Ruhhhhhh …” It was terrible!

“I think the girls can hear that,” said Toby. “So this time they can’t say we’re crazy!” We stayed in our sleeping bags, too scared to move. “Listen …” whispered Toby. “Can you hear a dog?”

18 **out there** da draußen

"A dog?"

"Yes. It's barking," said Toby. "On the other side of the hill. Listen."

"Yes, I can!" I whispered. "Isn't that Sheppy? Up at Home Farm?"

"Yes … I think it is!"

"It's strange," I said. "But last night I could hear Sheppy, too. She was barking right before we heard the noises …"

"Mmmm …" said Toby. "Maybe she knows something's not right …"

Just then, a strange thing happened. Somebody turned off the gas lamp! Suddenly, it was totally dark!

"Oh no!" whispered Toby. "W-Who did that?"

"One of the girls perhaps … ?" I said.

We stayed in our sleeping bags until we saw the first morning light. It was so good to see the sun after that terrible night! The girls came out of their tent, too.

"We heard the noise and we saw the shadow!" they said.

There were the same white hairs on the grass and on our tents.

"The creature has been here again," said Toby.

"The creature, the creature … You're always talking about the creature!" said Kelly.

"Well, somebody or something turned off the gas light!" I said.

"Nobody turned it off. It was just the wind," said Kelly.

"But there was no wind last night," Toby said.

8	**right before**	gerade bevor …
11	**just then**	in dem Moment, gerade dann
11	**turn off**	ausmachen, ausdrehen
12	**totally** ['təʊtəlɪ] **dark**	völlig dunkel

"Well ... how do you know the lamp had enough gas, Sherlock Holmes?" said Kelly, angry.

"We bought it at Home Farm yesterday, Watson! Remember?" Toby took the camping gas lamp. "Look!" he shouted. "Somebody *has* turned this thing off!"

"I've had enough of this!" said Lucy. "I'm going! This is too spooky for me!" And she started to pack her things in her rucksack. "Creatures in the night, strange noises, shadows, weirdos ... !"

"Come here!" I shouted from behind our tent. "Come and see this!" Kelly, Toby and Lucy came over to me. On the grass there was something red.

"B-blood ... ?!" said Lucy. Yes, there was red blood on our tent. Lucy ran back to pack her rucksack.

"Ow!" we heard her cry. We all ran to her. She was sitting on the grass.

"Lucy! Are you okay?"

"Oh, I've hurt my knee!" she answered. "I fell over your silly trainers, Toby! Why do you always leave your things around?"

"What are you talking about, Lucy?" said Toby, "I didn't leave my trainers there! Look! I'm wearing them!" Lucy stopped. We all stopped. There, on the grass, between the tents, were *my trainers*! But who put them there?

"I ... I don't like this," said Toby. "I'm going, too!"

Just then, the French family came by in their car with their caravan. They all looked very worried. The father was

11	**come over**	herüberkommen
13	**blood** [blʌd]	Blut
26	**come by**	vorbeikommen, -fahren
27	**worried** ['wʌrɪd]	besorgt, ängstlich

talking with his hands. He said something in French. We couldn't understand him because it was so fast. But we knew he was talking about the creature because he said again and again, "Furry ... furry!" And he made the terrible noise like the creature: "Ruhhhhhh! ... Shhhhh ... !" He laughed but he looked really scared. Then he said something like "Go before ... it is ... too late! Before it is ... too late!" And they drove away very fast.

Toby and Lucy wanted to go and find another camping site. They said they just wanted to hike and have picnics, and swim and have barbecues and sing songs by the campfire and do all the things people do on normal camping holidays. But my sister Kelly wanted to stay at Home Farm camping site and investigate.

8 **they drove** [drəʊv] **away** sie fuhren weg

"Somebody just wants to scare us," she said. "I'm going to stay and find out who it is!"

"This is just an adventure for you, Kelly," said Lucy. "But it could be dangerous!"

"Are you chicken?" Kelly asked us.

"Yes!" said Toby.

"What about you, James?" asked Kelly. "Do you want to go and find another camping site with these two? Or stay and investigate this thing? Somebody put that blood there! Remember: if we go, they win!"

2	**find out who it is**	herausfinden, wer das ist
5	**chicken** *(informal)*	*hier:* feige
10	**win**	gewinnen

Chapter 4: We investigate

We stayed. But Lucy and Toby were not very happy. We cleaned the blood on the tent. Then we went to investigate the place where the French family had their caravan. We looked on the grass and around the tree. We climbed the tree, too. But there were no white hairs there. And no blood. So why were the French family so scared? Why did they drive away so fast? *'Before it is too late?'* Did they really hear something in the night?

"Silly people look for creatures and monsters and ghosts, and they always see them," said Kelly. "But there's nothing there.That family was silly!"

"Why do you think so, Kelly?" I asked.

"Well, it's something I saw on their caravan.When they drove away this morning …" she said.

"Something on their caravan?"

"Yes," she said. "A sticker."

"F for France?" said Toby. "What is so special about that?"

"No, silly! Another sticker," said Kelly. "Didn't you see it, Lucy?"

"Yes, I think so … " said Lucy.

"Well, what did it say?" I asked.

" *'We have seen the Loch Ness Monster'* ".

"Yes, I saw that, too!" I remembered. "And there was something on the father's red cap too: *Bigfoot lives!*"

11 **nothing** ['nʌθɪŋ] nichts
25 **Bigfoot** legendäres Monster im Nordwesten der USA

We all laughed. It was good to laugh for the first time. Perhaps the French family *were* silly or crazy; they looked very strange when they drove away.

With the binoculars, we could see the other side of the lake; the weirdo's tent was open. Kelly wanted to investigate there too, perhaps ask him a few questions. But we thought it was a crazy idea. The weirdo could be dangerous. But Kelly liked to play Sherlock Holmes.

"I want to know what's going on," she said. "If you're all too chicken, I can do it alone!" Of course, we followed her.

It was a very small tent. There was a rucksack outside, some knives and some things for cooking on the grass next to the campfire. The weirdo was sitting on a small camping chair, with his back to us, and he was fishing in the lake. He had grey hair under a dirty old fisherman's cap. He looked old. Kelly said she wasn't chicken, but we knew she was scared. She spoke first.

"Ex-excuse me?"

The weirdo did not turn round. He did not move. Perhaps he did not hear her.

"Excuse me!" Kelly said it loud now. "Do you know anything about … a pair of trainers?" No answer. We waited.

8	**she liked to play**	sie spielte gern
15	**back**	*hier:* Rücken
16	**grey** [greɪ]	grau
18	**she spoke** [spəʊk]	sie sprach
20	**turn round**	sich umdrehen

"Excuse me," I said. "Have you … heard strange noises in the night?" We waited again.

But the old fisherman never turned round and he never answered us.

"Great!" said Toby when we got back to our tent. "That was really interesting!"

We went up to Home Farm. Bart was there alone. He didn't say hello. We said we wanted to buy some milk, but we really wanted to ask him some questions and get some more information.

"Somebody turned off our lamp in the night," we told him.

"Perhaps it was the wind," he said. "That happens."

"Somebody brought my trainers back, too," I said. "I found them behind my tent."

"Perhaps you just forgot where you put them," Bart answered. "I'm always losing things."

We told him too that the French family drove away fast and said '*Go before it's too late*'.

"Really?" he said. "They said that? But how … ?"

"We think they heard the strange noise, too," said Lucy. "And saw something … something white and furry!"

"Really?" said Bart.

I had a question: "Why did you tell us that old man is a weirdo? He looks like an old fisherman to me. We spoke to him but he didn't answer us."

"Don't speak to him again!" said Bart. "I told you – he's dangerous!"

Just then the farmer came back with Sheppy and Bart had to go for the milk.

"Hi, city kids!" the farmer shouted. "Did you sleep well, last night? No more furry monsters?" He laughed. "If you need more camping gas, just tell me. It can be very dark in the country."

"The camping gas is okay," said Kelly. She looked at us.

"I see you've found your trainers, my boy!" the farmer said to me.

"Well … they found me," I said.

Sheppy was jumping up on us. She knew us now.

"Down, Sheppy!" the farmer said.

"It's okay, we like dogs," we said.

"Sheppy follows me everywhere I go," he said. "I always have to take her with me. If I leave her in the house, she barks and barks."

This was interesting information.

"Yes, we know," said Toby. "We heard her … last night. And the night before." Just then, Sheppy ran to Bart in the barn.

"You see? She follows Bart now, too. When she knows you, she wants to follow you everywhere, silly dog!"

Lucy said, "I have a question … about the weirdo."

"The who?" said the farmer.

"You know, the old man in the tent on the other side of the lake …"

"Oh, Mr Conrad?" said the farmer.

"Well, we tried to speak to him this morning, but he didn't …"

"You spoke to Mr Conrad?" said the farmer.

"Yes, but he didn't answer us! He was fishing in the lake and he never turned round."

2 **no more monsters** keine Monster mehr

"That doesn't surprise me," said the farmer. "You see, old Mr Conrad is ..."

Suddenly, there was a loud crash! Bart had come back with our two bottles of milk and dropped them. There was milk everywhere.

"Oh no!" said the farmer.

"I'm sorry! That was Sheppy!" said Bart. "She jumped up on me! You're a bad dog, Sheppy!"

"Get fresh milk for the kids, Bart, and then clean this up! Quick!" said the farmer.

Bart went for more milk.

1 **surprise** [sə'praɪz]	überraschen
3 **he had come back**	er war zurückgekommen
5 **everywhere** ['evrɪhweə]	überall

"He's no help, that boy! And I must go and feed the rabbits," said the farmer. "Happy camping, kids!" Sheppy followed him.

That afternoon we had a meeting in our tent. Kelly still thought it was the farmer because he always laughed and called us 'city kids'. Toby thought it was Bart. "I think he knows something," he said. Lucy didn't like the weirdo because he didn't answer us, and his clothes and fisherman's cap were old and dirty … And I didn't know. But I had a plan to find out.

"Listen!" I said and took my camera from my rucksack. "This camera has got remote control. So I can put it right next to the door of the tent, and if we hear something in the night, I just take a picture. From inside the tent!"

"But you can't take pictures. It's too dark out there, James," said Lucy.

"No problem! This camera has got a flash."

"Wow!" they all said. "Great idea!"

"Then we can see who or what it is!" I said. "A big, wild, furry creature …"

"The farmer …" said Kelly.

"The weirdo …" said Lucy.

"Young Bart …" said Toby.

"The Frenchman …" I said. "Or perhaps a ghost!"

"Shhh …" whispered Kelly. "What's that?" It was only three o'clock in the afternoon, but somebody or something was outside the tent. We opened the tent door as fast as we could. Nothing!

6 **call** [kɔːl] *hier:* nennen
17 **flash** [flæʃ] Blitz(gerät)

"Somebody was here!" said Kelly. "I know it! Somebody was listening to us!"

We looked behind the tents and in the woods next to the field. Suddenly, Toby had something in his hand.

"Look what I found!" he shouted. "He dropped this!" Toby ran to us. In his hand was a cap!

"So it was *him*!" I said. "It was *him* all the time! Now we know!"

Kelly looked at the cap and said, "Well, we've got his cap! Now we need his picture!"

Chapter 5: The plan

That night it was really foggy. Toby turned off the gas lamp outside and got into our tent with Kelly, Lucy and me.

“Is everything ready out there?” we asked.

“Just like in the plan!” Toby said. We all waited in the tent in total darkness. I had the camera at the door of the tent and I took the remote control in my hand. We were all scared and excited too. We waited and waited in the dark. Was he going to come again? Then, just after twelve o’clock, we heard Sheppy. She was barking up at Home Farm. And ten minutes later, we heard some sounds outside the tent. Our ‘creature’ was walking around. Then the strange noises started: “Ruhhhhh … Ruhhhhhh … !” So he thought he could scare us with those silly creature noises, huh? I pressed the remote control. There was a flash! Then another! Flash! Then two more! Flash! Flash! There was a loud crash and the sound of broken glass as he fell over in the dark. Our plan was working! He couldn’t see a thing! Then he moved away fast into the woods.

“We have him!” I shouted. “Hurray!”

In the morning, outside the tent, we found a bucket of blood on its side. There were a lot of pieces of broken glass too. They looked like the pieces of a mirror.

7 **excited** [ɪk'saɪtɪd]	aufgeregt
14 **press**	drücken
16 **broken** ['brəʊkən]	gebrochen, zerbrochen
17 **work**	*hier:* funktionieren
24 **mirror** ['mɪrə]	Spiegel

"Ha!" shouted Toby. "He couldn't see a thing with all those flashes! He fell over our rucksacks in the dark! That was a great idea to put them there!" We all laughed. Now we weren't scared of chicken blood. And we knew the white hair was only from a rabbit. But why was there a broken mirror? We had no idea.

We ran to the bus stop to get the bus into Eastbourne. We waited for one hour outside the photo shop, and then we went in and collected our pictures. I opened the packet as fast as I could. In the first picture we saw ... nothing! It was all white! The second picture: all white too! The third was the same but we could just see a hand.

"Quick!" said Kelly. "Let's see the last photo!" In the last picture we could see him clearly. He had a bucket in his hand and he looked very scared!

"We're lucky to have one good photo," said Toby. "But why are the other photos all white?"

"Because he heard us yesterday, when we had our meeting in the tent," said Lucy. "Don't you see? He heard James's plan about the flash ..."

"He's not silly," I said. "That was a good idea with the mirror. And it almost worked. But when he fell over our rucksacks in the dark, he dropped it, and it broke. So we can see his silly face in this last picture. We have him now!"

Toby had the cap he found in the woods that afternoon. Now he took it from his pocket. *Chicago Bulls.* Now we had everything!

9	**collect**	*hier:* holen
14	**clearly** ['klɪəlɪ]	klar, deutlich
27	**pocket**	Tasche

When we told the farmer, he didn't really believe us. Then we showed him the photograph, the bucket of chicken blood, a piece of the broken mirror and the baseball cap. He was very angry with Bart and sent him home. We watched as Bart got into a taxi and left Home Farm. He had a big white bandage on his head and another bandage on his arm. He did not look at us.

"That's what happens when you break a mirror and then fall on it!" whispered Toby.

"I don't want him here now!" the farmer said.

The taxi drove away with Bart in it.

"You kids never really believed it was a creature, did you?" asked the farmer.

"Oh, no, never!" we all said together.

"So you knew it was Bart all the time?" he asked.

"Well, we thought it could be many different people. You too!" We all laughed.

"Me?" said the farrner. "Why did you think it was me? I don't want to scare away my campers!"

"Well, how did you know James had trainers? Not sandals or shoes or boots?"

"I *didn't* know," he answered. "But all kids wear trainers now. Look! It's true. You're all wearing them!"

"Well, there's one thing I still don't understand," said Lucy. "When we spoke to the weirdo … sorry, the old fisherman in the tent, next to the lake …"

"Mr Conrad?"

"Yes, he didn't answer us."

1 **believe** [bɪ'li:v] glauben

"That doesn't surprise me," said the farmer. "Old Mr Conrad is totally deaf. He didn't hear you, that's all."

"Oh, I see," said Lucy.

"Yes, Mr Conrad's a nice old man. He camps here at Home Farm every summer. He likes to fish in the lake."

"But ... why is his tent closed up every night? There's no light on ..."

"That's because he goes to bed with the sun and gets up with the sun! But what did Bart tell you about Mr Conrad?"

"Oh ... nothing really," we said. We all felt very silly because we believed Bart's stories.

"I don't understand one last thing," I said. "The French family. They packed up their caravan and they looked so scared when they drove away. There was no furry creature, so why were they so scared?"

"The Dulac family?" said the farmer. "I really don't know ..."

"Well, they heard *something*," said Toby. "Because the father could make a noise just like the creature ... just like Bart. You know: Ruhhhhh ... Sshhhhh ..."

"And they said: '*Go before it is too late*'," said Kelly. "Why did they drive away so fast?"

"Well, I only know they were very late for the one o'clock ferry," said the farmer. "You know, the ferry-boat. Back to France ..."

"Oh!" we all said. "He was saying *ferry*!"

"Well, what did you kids think he was saying?"

2 **deaf** [def] taub
25 **ferry** Fähre

After that, our camping holiday really started. At last, we could do all the normal things. We hiked in the hills, had picnics and swam to the other side of the lake. We learned to talk to old Mr Conrad. He wasn't a weirdo at all; he was a great old man. We all went on the lake in his little boat and fished. One evening, we had a great fish barbecue at his tent. Kelly played her guitar and we sang songs around the campfire.

Now, when Kelly and I, and Toby and Lucy talk about that holiday, we have to laugh. Did we really believe there was a creature in the night? Were we really so silly?

THE END

3 **they swam** sie schwammen
4 **(not) at all** überhaupt (nicht)

Activities

Before you read

1. Have you camped? Where did you go camping? Who did you go camping with?
2. What can you do on a camping holiday?
   You can have a barbecue ... sleep in a tent ... hike ... etc.
3. What can be bad on a camping holday?
   rain? *wild animals?* *the dark?* ...?

Chapter 1

1. How do you "see" the camping site in your head? *Draw it.
2. Write the *past tense* of these verbs. You can find them all in Chapter 1.

a) sit *sat*	d) light	g) say ....
b) sing	e) get (into)	h) know ....
c) feel	f) hear	i) think ....

3. Complete this text with the verbs from exercise 2. (You do not need them all!)
   At night, it was dark, so we .... the lamp and .... into our sleeping bags. Suddenly, we .... a strange noise outside. 'That must be Sheppy, the farmer's dog,' we .... But we .... she was at Home Farm, so it could not be her. Then we .... a shadow and we .... very scared.

draw zeichnen

Chapter 2

1. Look at the map of Home Farm on the inside cover. How do the kids get to Home Farm from the camping site?
   They go out of / They leave …
   They walk along …
   They turn …
   They go up …

2. The farmer says these things about the creature. Right or wrong? If it's wrong, write the correct answer in your exercise book.
   a) *Some people say there's a creature in this part of the country.*
   b) *I have seen the creature!*
   c) *It comes in the morning.*
   d) *It only steals sheep.*
   e) *The creature is more than seven feet tall.*
   f) *It's furry and black.*

3. What do *you* think the creature looks like? Draw it. (Information in the text can help you.)

4. What do you learn about the *weirdo*? Write a short text about him. These words can help you:

sleep
walk around
lake
dangerous
at night
no light on
tent
camping site

Chapter 3

1. *Before you read*
   Look at the *title* of this chapter. Who is going to have the dream? What is going to happen in the dream? What do you think? Now read Chapter 3.

2. Which words from the left can go together with words from the right?

camping sleeping walking wild chicken cheese flat farm baseball	burgers cap animal site bag boots sandwiches gas lamp

3. Work in small groups. Copy the friends' *dialogue* with the French family (pages 16 –18) into your exercise book. Choose a part and read the dialogue together. You can learn your part and act it too!

Chapter 4

1. What countries have these car stickers?

(I) (F) (GB) (D) (E)

(CH) (P) (NL) (A)

Example: (F) = France

2. What is it?
   a) The friends can see the other side of the lake with these. *binoculars*
   b) James found this on the tent. It's red. ....
   c) Somebody did this to the gas lamp in the night. ....
   d) It's a long walk in the hills. ....
   e) The friends feel this when they hear strange noises. ....
   f) They do this when they see the French family. It's like 'hello'. ....
   g) It flies, it lives in trees and it makes a noise at night. ....
   h) The French family live in one. ....
   i) Some people make this noise when they sleep. ....
   j) It's on a farm. Animals live in it. ....

3. The friends think the noises in the night could be:

   the creature – the weirdo – the Frenchman
   the farmer – Bart

   Who thinks what? Why?
   Kelly thinks it's ... because ...
   Who do *you* think it is? Why?

4. Who wears which cap?
   a) Draw the four caps in the story, for example, the farmer's flat cap; Bart's cap ...
   b) Which cap do the friends find in the woods? What do *you* think?

Chapter 5

1. Complete these sentences.
   a) Bart had bandages on his head and arm because …
   b) Old Mr Conrad didn't answer the kids' questions because …
   c) The French family left the camping site fast because ...

2. Put these sentences in the correct order.
   a) The next morning we found blood on the tent.
   b) We arrived at Home Farm.
   c) Bart had to leave Home Farm.
   d) We heard strange noises and saw a shadow.
   e) Somebody stole James's trainers.
   f) We had a meeting and made a plan.
   g) We took pictures with James's camera.
   h) We found Bart's baseball cap, so we knew it was him.
   i) That night somebody turned off our gas lamp.
   j) At Home Farm we heard about the weirdo and the creature.

3. Complete these sentences. Who says them?
   a) 'That's what happens when you break a mirror and then … on it'. ....
   b) 'I've had enough of this! I'm going! This is too … for me!' ....
   c) 'Go before it's too … !' ....
   d) 'Remember, if we go, they … ! ....
   e) 'You city kids are just scared of the … !' ....
   f) 'No more furry …?' ....
   g) 'You mustn't talk to him! He's … !' ....
   h) 'How can I be ...? I'm not sleeping!' ....

   Example:
   c) 'Go before it's too **late**!' *The Frenchman says this.*